The Sun

by Grace Hansen

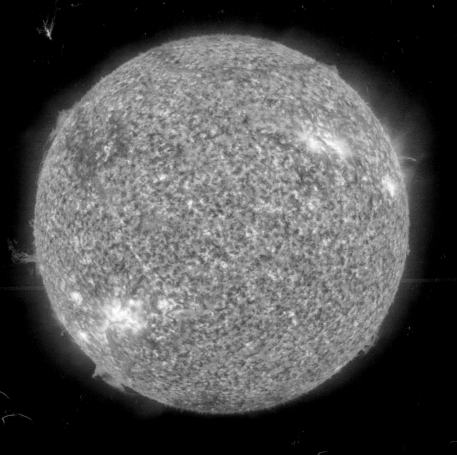

Abdo
OUR GALAXY
Kids

abdopublishing.com

Published by Abdo Kids, a division of ABDO, P.O. Box 398166, Minneapolis, Minnesota 55439.

Printed in the United States of America, North Mankato, Minnesota.

052017

092017

 THIS BOOK CONTAINS
RECYCLED MATERIALS

Photo Credits: iStock, NASA, Shutterstock

Production Contributors: Teddy Borth, Jennie Forsberg, Grace Hansen

Design Contributors: Dorothy Toth, Laura Mitchell

Publisher's Cataloging in Publication Data

Names: Hansen, Grace, author.

Title: The sun / by Grace Hansen.

Description: Minneapolis, Minnesota : Abdo Kids, 2018 | Series: Our galaxy |
    Includes bibliographical references and index.

Identifiers: LCCN 2016962472 | ISBN 9781532100543 (lib. bdg.) |
    ISBN 9781532101236 (ebook) | ISBN 9781532101786 (Read-to-me ebook)

Subjects: LCSH: Sun--Juvenile literature.

Classification: DDC 523.7--dc23

LC record available at http://lccn.loc.gov/2016962472

Table of Contents

How the Sun Was Made

Our **solar system** formed around 4.6 billion years ago. That means our sun is about 4.6 billion years old.

5

The sun formed out of a giant cloud of dust and gas. At some point, strong waves of energy hit the cloud. This caused the cloud to press together.

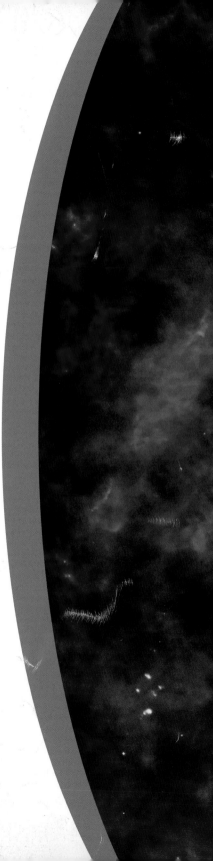

The cloud got denser. Gravity took over and the cloud began to collapse. The cloud began to spin and form a disc.

9

As the disc spun faster, it pulled more material toward the center. The material at the center became so hot that **hydrogen fused** into **helium**. This made a huge amount of energy. And the sun was born!

The Sun

The sun is a star. It is the closest star to Earth. This is why it looks so much bigger than other stars in the sky.

13

The sun also looks big because it is big! It is 870,000 miles (1,400,130 km) in diameter. About 1.3 million Earths could fit inside the sun!

Earth

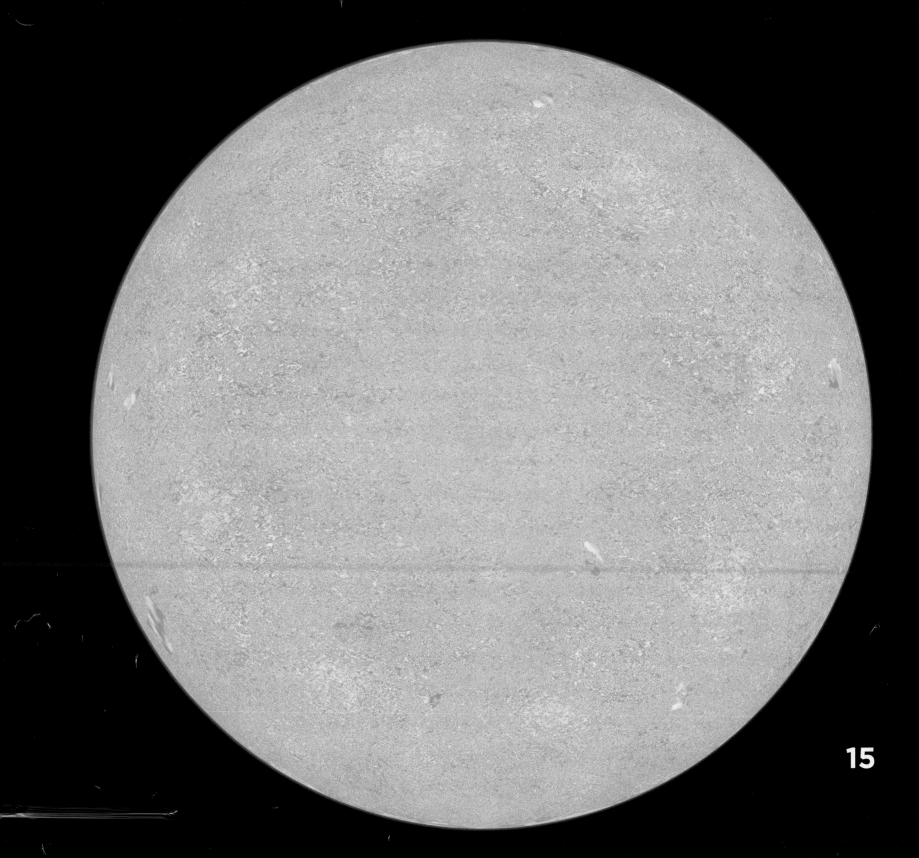

15

The sun makes up 99.86% of the mass of our **solar system**. So its **gravitational** pull is very strong. That is why the planets rotate around the sun.

Saturn

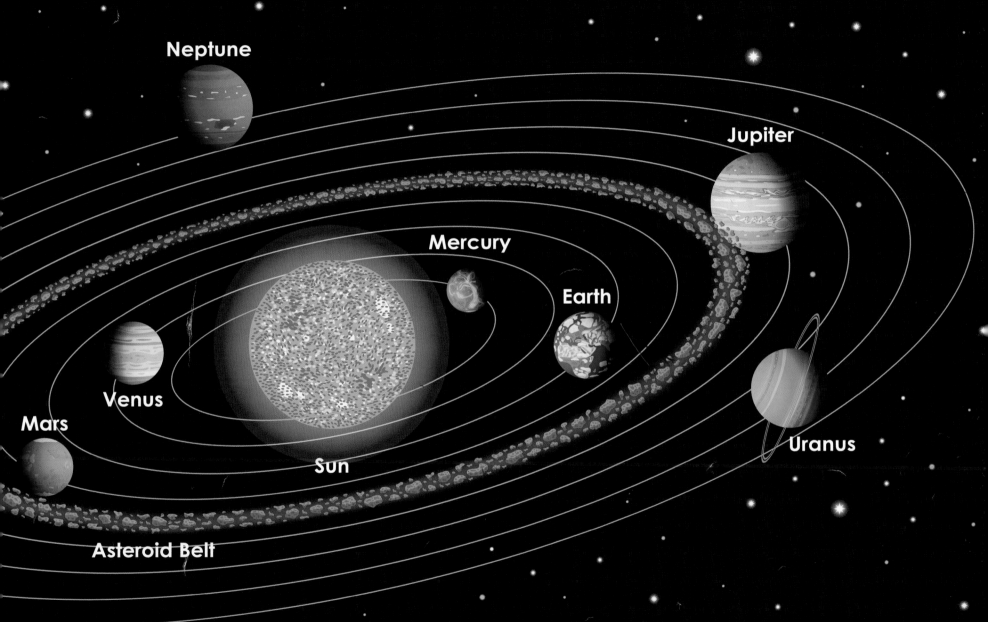

Neptune

Jupiter

Mercury

Earth

Venus

Mars

Sun

Uranus

Asteroid Belt

17

The sun is made up of many layers. The **core** makes up the center of the sun. The part of the sun we can see is called the photosphere.

core

photosphere

Life

The sun creates energy every second of every day. We rely on the sun's heat and light. The sun makes life on Earth possible.

More Facts

- Light from the sun takes eight minutes to reach Earth.

- Our sun is currently in the middle of its life. It has about 5 billion years to live.

- When the sun is nearing the end of its life it will swell up to become a red giant. When this happens, Mercury, Venus, and even Earth could be absorbed by the giant sun!

Glossary

core – the center of a star where the temperature and pressures are great enough to ignite nuclear fusion, converting atoms of hydrogen into helium.

dense – packed close together.

fusion – combining the nucleuses of many atoms to create a huge amount of energy.

gravity – the force by which all objects in the universe are attracted to each other.

helium – a light, colorless gas that does not burn.

hydrogen – a gas that is lighter than air and catches fire easily.

solar system – a group of planets and other celestial bodies that are held by the sun's gravity and revolve around it.

Index

abdokids.com

Use this code to log on to abdokids.com and access crafts, games, videos and more!

Abdo Kids Code:
OTK0543

CHARLIE BROWN'S CYCLOPEDIA

BOATS AND THINGS THAT FLOAT
All Aboard!

VOLUME · 10 ·

Based on the Charles M. Schulz Characters
Funk & Wagnalls

Photo and Illustration Credits:
AP/Wide World Photos, 47; Joe Azzara/Image Bank, 36; David Barnes/West Light, 42; Brent Bear/West Light, 47; The Bettmann Archive, 14, 22, 32; Robert Copeland/West Light, 18; E.R. Degginger/Earth Scenes, 13; Tom Edwards/Earth Scenes, 48; Lawrence Fried/Image Bank, 43; The Granger Collection, 24; David W. Hamilton/Image Bank, 57; T. Jacobi/Image Bank, 28; Bryce Lee, 12, 16, 18, 49, 54; Larry Lee/West Light, 27, 40, 45; R. Ian Lloyd/West Light, 44; Courtesy NOAA, 53; Charles O'Rear/West Light, 33, 41; Ralph A. Reinhold/Earth Scenes, 17; L.L.T. Rhodes/Earth Scenes, 58; Guido A. Rossi/Image Bank, 39; Cosimo Scianna/Image Bank, 51; Don A. Sparks/Image Bank, 30.

ISBN: 0-8374-0055-4

Part of the material in this volume was previously published in *Charlie Brown's Second Super Book of Questions and Answers.*

Funk & Wagnalls, founded in 1876, is the publisher of *Funk & Wagnalls New Encyclopedia,* one of the most widely owned home and school reference sets, and many other adult and juvenile educational publications.

INTRODUCTION

Welcome to volume 10 of *Charlie Brown's 'Cyclopedia!* Have you ever wondered what the first boats were like, or what a galleon is, or how an icebreaker works? Charlie Brown and the rest of the *Peanuts* gang are here to help you find the answers to these questions and many more about all kinds of boats and other things that float. Have fun!

Charlie Brown's 'Cyclopedia
has been produced
by Mega-Books of New York,
Inc. in conjunction
with the editorial, design,
and marketing staff of
Field Publications.

**STAFF FOR
MEGA-BOOKS**

Pat Fortunato
Editorial Director

Diana Papasergiou
Production Director

Susan Lurie
Executive Editor

Rosalind Noonan
Senior Editor

Adam Schmetterer
Research Director

**Michaelis/Carpelis
Design Assoc., Inc.**
Art Direction and Design

**STAFF FOR
FIELD PUBLICATIONS**

Cathryn Clark Girard
Assistant Vice President,
Juvenile Publishing

Elizabeth Isele
Executive Editor

Kristina Jorgensen
Executive Art Director

Leslie Erskine
Marketing Manager

Elizabeth Zuraw
Senior Editor

Michele Italiano-Perla
Group Art Director

Kathleen Hughes
Senior Art Director

CONTENTS

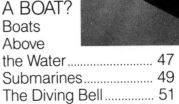

When you live near water, there's only one way to travel across it and stay dry—in a boat! Boats can cut through an ocean's high waves or skim across a calm lake. No matter how big or small your boat is, though, one thing is certain—it had better float!

ROW, ROW, ROW YOUR BOAT

CHAPTER 1

WHY BOATS FLOAT

What makes a boat float?

When something solid, such as a boat, is put into a liquid, such as water, the solid pushes some of the liquid aside. If the solid weighs more than the liquid it pushes aside, it will sink. If it weighs less, it will float. A huge, heavy ship floats even though it is made of steel. Because it contains a lot of air, it weighs less than the water it pushes aside. That is why it floats.

These arrows show how water presses against a hull to make a boat float.

Narrow boats move through water more quickly than wide boats because they have less water to push aside.

Why are most boats long and narrow?

Long, narrow boats can go through the water quickly. A force called "drag" holds back anything that moves through water. The wider the boat, the more drag there is, so a narrow boat can go faster than a wide one.

THE FIRST RAFTS

How did people first cross rivers and streams?

If the water was too deep to walk through, people probably swam, but only the strongest swimmers could have gotten across a wide river. Some early, tired swimmer probably grabbed onto a floating log. He or she became the first person to use a raft—a simple platform that floats on water.

What were early rafts like?

Once people realized that they could float on a log, they probably tied two logs together and then three logs and then four logs for bigger and bigger rafts. Soon people began to experiment with other types of rafts. In Egypt, for example, they tied together bundles of sticks or heavy reeds.

The earliest rafts were probably made of wood, much like this river craft.

How did people move their rafts?

At first, the raft rider had nothing to paddle with but his or her hands. Later, riders probably used a stick to push the raft through the water. Still later, people discovered that a flat piece of wood worked better than a stick. It made the raft go faster. That's how the paddle was invented.

Are there any famous rafts?

The *Kon-Tiki* is one of the most famous rafts in the world. It was built in 1947 by Thor Heyerdahl (HI-ur-doll), a Norwegian scientist. Heyerdahl sailed the tiny *Kon-Tiki* thousands of miles across the Pacific Ocean without any modern equipment. He went from South America to Polynesia (pol-uh-NEE-zhuh)—a group of islands south of Hawaii. Heyerdahl's voyage proved that people could have made the same trip by raft 1,500 years ago. It is possible, then, that the people of Polynesia are the great-, great-, great-grandchildren of South American Indians.

What did the *Kon-Tiki* look like?

The *Kon-Tiki* was a copy of the rafts used by natives of the South Pacific. It was made of balsa, a light wood that floats easily. It was 45 feet long and 18 feet wide. On the center of the raft was a bamboo cabin that Heyerdahl used for shelter.

The *Kon-Tiki* flew flags from several different nations, including the United States.

What were the first boats like?

The first boats developed from rafts. To keep dry, people turned up the sides of their reed rafts. In this way, they invented a boat that looked like a saucer, but these round boats were hard to steer. It didn't take long for people to learn to build longer, thinner boats. These were easier to steer and could move through the water much faster.

CANOES

What is a canoe?

A canoe is a long, narrow boat that is pointed at both ends. One, two, or three people sit in the canoe, facing the front, or bow (rhymes with *cow*). They use a paddle, or paddles, to move the canoe through the water and to steer it. Canoes were among the first kinds of small boats.

What did the earliest Americans use when they traveled by water?

Native Americans used canoes. They had two kinds, dugout and birchbark, depending on where they lived. In the north, where birch trees grew, Native Americans made birchbark canoes. In other places, they made dugouts.

How did the Native Americans make a dugout canoe?

A dugout canoe was made from a long, thick log. The canoe maker burned the middle of the log in order to make the wood soft, but had to be careful not to burn all the way through. Then the canoe maker scraped, or dug out, all the soft, burned wood to make the inside hollow.

Dugout canoes are very strong but slow. They're also heavy—too heavy to be carried far on land.

MOVE IT... MOVE IT. WHAT'S WRONG HERE?

WE ALL STEP TO THE SOUND OF A DIFFERENT DRUMMER.

What is a birchbark canoe?

A birchbark canoe is much lighter than a dugout canoe. It can be carried easily from one stream to another. These canoes are made from strips of bark peeled from birch trees. After building a frame out of wood, the canoe maker sews the strips together, using tree roots for thread. Then the canoe maker attaches the bark to the canoe's wooden frame.

Building a birchbark canoe

Are canoes still used today?

Yes. In certain places, such as Africa and the South Pacific Islands, people still travel by canoe. In most other parts of the world, however, canoes are used mainly for fun. People take them on fishing or camping trips. Today, most canoes are built by machine, and they are made of canvas, light metal, or plastic.

In 1928, a man crossed the Atlantic Ocean in a canoe with a sail. The trip took 58 days!

KAYAKS AND ROWBOATS

Kayaks weigh very little. Because they are so light, they move quickly through the water.

What is a kayak?

A kayak (KI-ak) is the canoe the Eskimos have been using for thousands of years. It is long and pointed like most canoes. Kayaks, however, are not open. Their top is covered, except for one small hole for the paddler. Most kayaks have room for only one paddler.

Some kayak paddles look like canoe paddles, but most are double-bladed, that is, they have a blade at each end. The paddler dips one blade into the water on the right side, then swings the paddle over and dips the other blade in on the left side.

How are kayaks made?

Kayaks are made in almost the same way as birchbark canoes. The Eskimos just use different materials. The frame of the kayak is made of wood or whalebone—the tough plates whales have instead of teeth. Sealskin is used for the outside. It is stretched tightly over the frame, leaving a small opening for the paddler.

Are kayaks always made of sealskin?

No. These days, most kayaks are made of light metal, wood, or plastic, just like canoes. Some kayaks and other small boats are made of heavy cloth that has rubber on one side. They must be pumped full of air, or inflated, before they will float. When there is no air in them, they can be folded up and stored in very small places. Kayaks and rubber rafts are used mostly for fun.

What is a rowboat?

A rowboat is any kind of boat that is moved by oars. An oar is longer than a paddle, but it's used the same way. The rower usually uses two oars, one on each side of the boat. To keep the oars from slipping into the water, they are held in place by oarlocks on the sides of the boat.

Rowboats tied to a dock

Did boats ever have more than two oars?

Yes. When people started building large ships, they needed many oars to move them. A galley, one of the earliest ships, sometimes had 50 or more oars.

Galleys were first used by the people who lived around the Mediterranean (med-ih-tuh-RAY-nee-un) Sea more than 3,000 years ago. Many of these people were from Egypt and Phoenicia (foh-NISH-uh), the land where Syria, Lebanon, and Israel are today.

Galleys were rowed by slaves who sat on benches. Each man held an oar with both hands. All the slaves rowed at once, to the beat of a drum. Most galleys also had one large oar at the back of the boat. It was used for steering.

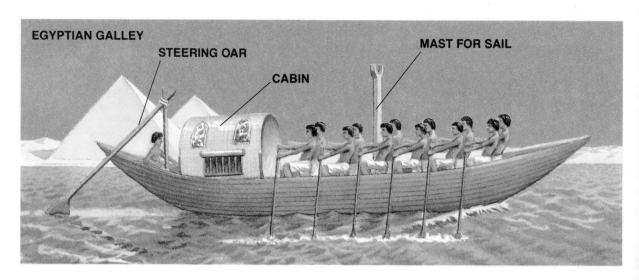

EGYPTIAN GALLEY

STEERING OAR

CABIN

MAST FOR SAIL

What was the biggest galley ship?

The biggest galley ship was made in Alexandria, Egypt. It was 420 feet long and could carry 4,000 rowers. Eight men were needed to handle each 57-foot oar. Built more than 2,000 years ago, this giant galley was the largest ship to be powered by humans.

Early Romans believed that ships needed eyes to see. So they painted eyes on their galleys!

What's the difference between boats and ships?

Boats are smaller than ships, and they rarely travel far out on the ocean. Ships do. They are large, seagoing vessels. Ships are used for trading, carrying passengers, and fighting battles.

CHAPTER 2

Captain Brown and his merry crew are here to take you on a super sailboat journey. If we catch the wind just right, there'll be smooth sailing ahead! You won't need a paddle or an engine—just a tall sail and the mighty wind. Let's go!

CATCHING THE WIND

EARLY SAILBOATS

Why did people add sails to their boats?

A sail on a boat can catch the wind. This, in turn, causes the boat to move. The ancient Egyptians discovered this fact about 5,000 years ago. The first sails were made of thick materials that could trap the wind. Sailboat builders used a large piece of linen or papyrus (puh-PIE-russ)—a heavy, coarse paper.

   The early sailors could travel only *with* the wind. If the wind was blowing in the wrong direction, they had to put down their sails and row the boat. It was not until the triangular sail was invented that sailing in almost any direction became possible. This happened about 1,600 years ago.

Who were the first sailors to use ships?

The Egyptians started to do a great deal of sailing more than 4,000 years ago. They made easy-to-sail ships from wooden boards. They sailed these ships around the Mediterranean, trading with other countries. Then, about 3,000 years ago, the Phoenicians began to design ships both for trading and for fighting sea battles. They made long, fast ships for fighting and short, wide ones for trading.

Were there galley ships with sails?

Although the first galleys had no sails, later ones did. Even so, their most important source of power was muscle. Sails helped the galleys move, but they still needed oars.

Who thought of using more than one sail?

About 2,500 years ago, both the Greeks and the Phoenicians came up with a new idea in ship design. Until then, ships had always had one mast—a pole for a sail—and one sail. The Greeks and Phoenicians added a second mast and two more sails. The new sails gave them extra speed and better control. About 2,000 years later, the Greeks added a third mast and a fourth sail.

THE VIKINGS

Who were the Vikings?

The Vikings were fierce seagoing pirates from Norway, Sweden, and Denmark. They raided Europe by sea about 1,000 years ago, and probably reached North America before Christopher Columbus did. The Vikings settled in areas that now are England, Russia, Iceland, and Greenland.

This painting shows Viking ships sailing through rough seas.

The Vikings founded the city of Dublin, Ireland!

What kind of ships did the Vikings use?

The Vikings used trading ships and warships. The trading ships were called *knorrs* (pronounce the *k*). The knorrs were very wide and carried goods for trading. They didn't have many oars, so there was a lot of room for cargo.

What were the warships like?

Viking warships were long, narrow, and fast. They had many oars and just one sail. The earliest of these were called long ships. Later, the Vikings built ships that were longer than the long ships! Each of these later ships had a wooden carving at the front. This carving, called a figurehead, was of a person or a monster, such as a dragon. Because the figurehead was often a dragon, the Vikings called these warships *drakkars*, which means "dragons."

Why did Vikings put figureheads on their ships?

Some figureheads served the same purpose as a name painted on a ship. They were used to identify the ship. The Vikings also believed figureheads scared away evil spirits. That's why carvings of dragon heads and monsters were common on Viking ships.

Why is the right side of a ship called starboard and the left called port?

The Vikings were the first to use those names. A typical Viking ship had a giant steering oar. It was on the right side, near the back of the ship. It was there for two reasons. First, most people are right-handed. Second, the ancient people believed that the right side of a ship was stronger than the left side. The right side of a Viking ship was eventually called the "steerboard." Over the years the word changed a little, to starboard.

Because the steering oar was in the way, the Vikings could not dock on the right side of the ship. They always docked with the left side facing port. So that's what they called it—and so do we.

EXPLORING WITH CHRISTOPHER COLUMBUS

Why did Columbus sail west to get to the East?

Christopher Columbus believed that the world was round. Before his time (the late 1400s), just about everyone had assumed that the world was flat. If the world really was round, Columbus thought, he should be able to reach the Indies—east of Europe—by sailing west. *The Indies* was a name for India, China, and the islands of Southeast Asia. In fact, Columbus believed the shortest route to be west across the Atlantic Ocean.

Columbus's biggest ship, the *Santa María*, probably looked like this.

When Columbus reached America for the first time, he thought he was in the Indies. That's why he named the people there Indians!

What kind of ships did Christopher Columbus use for his famous 1492 voyage?

Two of Columbus's ships, the *Niña* and the *Pinta*, were caravels. These light, fast sailing ships first became popular around 1400. They had three masts: the foremast (in the front), the mainmast (in the middle), and the mizzenmast (in the back). The foremast had a square sail. The other two masts had sails in the shape of triangles.

The third ship—and the largest—was a carrack. Known as the *Santa María*, it was the one Columbus himself traveled on. The ship had the same three masts as the caravels, but both the mainmast and the foremast had square sails. Only the mizzenmast had a sail in the shape of a triangle. A pole called a bowsprit stuck out from the front, or bow, of the ship. It held a small square sail.

FERDINAND MAGELLAN

Who was the first person to sail around the world?

Ferdinand Magellan always gets the credit, although he never actually completed the trip around the world. However, one of his ships did.

In 1519, Magellan decided to try to find a short route to the Indies. He planned to go around the tip of South America and then west to Asia.

Magellan left Spain with five ships. In two years, he got halfway around the world, but during the voyage, he was killed on a Pacific island. Of his five ships, four didn't complete the trip. One ship was wrecked on a rock. One returned to Spain early. One was left, leaking badly, on a Pacific island. One was lost. Only one ship completed the trip.

Where did Columbus's crew sleep?

On the floor! Only the most important officers of the *Niña*, the *Pinta*, and the *Santa María* slept in bunks. The other men slept on deck. However, after the first voyage to America, the crew slept below deck in hammocks. The hammock was a Native American invention that Columbus's men adopted.

WELL, HE ALMOST MADE IT!

THE SPANISH ARMADA

What was the Spanish Armada?

For many years, no country was as mighty as Spain when it came to ocean travel. During the 1500s, Spain had the largest fleet of ships in Europe. The fleet was known as the Spanish Armada. These ships were used by Spanish explorers to sail across the Atlantic Ocean to America. The Spaniards brought back many treasures from the New World, making Spain very rich.

The Armada also protected Spain from enemies and fought her battles when it was necessary. Because of its Armada, Spain was, for many years, one of the most powerful countries in Europe. In 1588, however, a fleet of English ships defeated the Armada. England became mistress of the sea.

The mighty Spanish Armada included 130 ships of war, 8,000 sailors, and 20,000 soldiers!

What is a galleon?

A galleon is a large wooden sailing ship that was popular in Europe during the mid-1500s. It was used for trading and, in wartime, for battle. A galleon was better for long-distance sea voyages than earlier ships. It was deeper, so it had bunk space for the whole crew.

The foremast and the mainmast of a galleon each had two or three sails. Sometimes the mizzenmast had two sails, also. Some of the early galleons had oars as well as sails, but galleons could be rowed only in smooth waters.

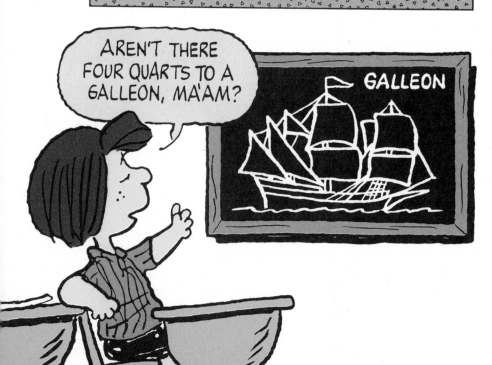

THE MAYFLOWER

What kind of ship was the *Mayflower*?

The ship that carried the Pilgrims to the New World in 1620 was a fairly small trading ship. She was about 90 feet—as long as six cars lined up in a row. Some passengers on the *Mayflower* slept in bunks along the sides of the ship. Others made their beds on the floor of the covered deck. The upper part of the ship leaked, so the Pilgrims often felt ice-cold water splashing on them.

Before she carried passengers, the *Mayflower* had carried wine. Because of that, the ship's hold—the place where the cargo is kept—smelled quite sweet. Most other ships of that time smelled of garbage and damp cargo.

A model of the *Mayflower* sits in the waters off Massachusetts.

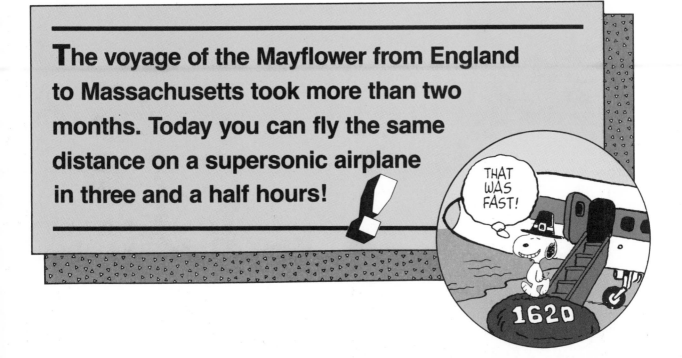

The voyage of the Mayflower from England to Massachusetts took more than two months. Today you can fly the same distance on a supersonic airplane in three and a half hours!

THAT WAS FAST!

1620

SCHOONERS, CLIPPER SHIPS, AND WINDJAMMERS

THREE-MASTED SCHOONER

What is a schooner?

A schooner is a large sailboat. It was popular as a fishing boat in New England in the 1700s. In those days, it had from two to seven masts. Although schooners aren't used much today, some still exist. Most of these have two or three masts and are used mostly for fun.

What were the fastest sailing ships?

Clipper ships were the fastest and the most beautiful sailing ships. Their beauty and speed came from the way they were built. They had long, sleek bodies and lots of sails. Some had as many as 35 sails.

Clipper ships were used during the mid-1800s. At that time, the United States and East Asia, especially China, were doing a great deal of trading. Clippers carried tea, coffee, and spices. These products would spoil if they remained on board ship for too long, so speed was very important. Clipper ships were named for the way they could "clip off the miles." A clipper could travel from the east coast of the United States to China and back in six months.

Clipper ships were the fastest sailing ships.

What were windjammers?

Windjammers were iron sailing ships with four masts. They became popular just after clipper ships. They, too, were used for trading and carrying cargo. Windjammers were huge and strong, perfect for sailing in bad weather and on rough seas.

Did any of these sailing ships carry passengers?

Almost all carried passengers as well as cargo. However, these ships sailed only when the weather was good, so passengers couldn't plan their trips ahead of time.

In the mid-1800s, packet ships became popular. They sailed at a set time, no matter what. The ship owners also made sure that first-class passengers were comfortable, so packet ships became very popular with rich ocean travelers.

RACING WITH THE WIND

What are racing sailboats made of?

Racing sailboats are very light and are made of wood, plastic, light metal, or fiberglass. They are fast and easy to handle. Modern sails are made of nylon or polyester, similar to the material of a windbreaker or winter jacket.

Are large sailboats ever used for racing?

Yes. For ocean racing, sailors must have a large boat. Because ocean races may be more than 1,300 miles long, the boats must be well built and able to handle rough waters. A boat called the 12-meter racer is the type most often used in the big race called the America's Cup. In 1988, however, the United States won the America's Cup with a type of sailboat called a catamaran.

What is a yacht?

The word *yacht* is used to describe sailing boats as small as a one-person, eight-foot dinghy to huge powerboats as long as 20 taxicabs in a row. Yachts can be used for pleasure cruising or full speed racing.

Dinghies and multihulls are two kinds of racing yachts. Each of these types of boats is built to guidelines for its particular group, or class. For each type of boat, there are many classes, based on length, sail size, and weight. Boat racers usually race against similar boats so that the race is a test of sailing skill, not of who has the biggest engine or largest sail.

These catamarans are locked in a close race!

What is a catamaran?

A catamaran is a sailboat with two separate hulls that are joined. A hull is the body, or frame, of a boat. In a catamaran, a little space is left between the hulls. "Cats," as these unusual-looking boats are called, are very fast. The two hulls cause less drag, making the cat a very fast boat.

Catamarans were invented by people who lived in the South Seas—a part of the Pacific Ocean. There, the natives used logs to make the two hulls. They used paddles and sometimes added sails to make their cats move. People still sail catamarans today.

owing and sailing can be lots of fun, but how can you make a boat move without oars or a breeze? Over the years, inventors have come up with a few ways to power boats. If you want to see how, then hold on. We're ready to move, full steam ahead!

FULL STEAM AHEAD

EARLY STEAMBOATS AND THE PADDLE WHEEL

When did people start using steamboats?

The first workable steamboat was built in 1787 by an American named John Fitch. The boat had six long paddles on each side—like an overgrown canoe! The boat's paddles got their power from a steam engine.

Three years later, Fitch improved his model and put the paddles at the back. He then started taking passengers and cargo up and down the Delaware River. However, the engine was so large that there was very little room for the cargo, and not many people were interested in traveling on such a noisy boat. Fitch's steamboat service failed.

What was Fulton's Folly?

In 1807, Robert Fulton built the *Clermont*, the first successful steamboat. At first, people thought that building a steamboat was foolish. They referred to the boat as "Fulton's Folly," but Fulton combined the best features from other steamboats. Soon, the *Clermont* was making regular trips along New York's Hudson River.

People laughed when Fulton first built the *Clermont*. After his steamboat became a success, Fulton had the last laugh!

Though the Clermont had room to seat 24 passengers, only 14 people were brave enough to go on its first trip. One month later, 90 passengers crowded on board!

What did the *Clermont* look like?

The *Clermont* was a long, thin boat. It had a smokestack that coughed out black smoke. Even though it had a steam engine, there were sails in case the engine broke down. It did not have canoe paddles like John Fitch's boat. Instead, the *Clermont* had a paddle wheel on each side.

A paddle-wheel boat churns through a river's water.

What is a paddle wheel?

A paddle wheel is a huge wheel with a series of flat paddles attached to it. Part of the wheel is always underwater. The power from a steam engine turns the wheel. As the paddles push the water, they move the boat forward.

Where were paddle-wheel boats used?

Paddle-wheel boats were used mostly on rivers. Sailboats move slowly on rivers because there isn't much wind there. Since paddle-wheel boats are powered by steam, not wind, they move quickly. Steamboats were popular on the Ohio and Mississippi rivers.

In 1986, a paddle-wheel boat was built from 40,000 milk cartons. The boat was named the Milky Wave and actually sailed with passengers!

What was a showboat?

A showboat was a paddle-wheel steamboat used as a traveling theater. In the 1800s, gaily decorated showboats brought plays, circuses, and live music to towns along the Mississippi River. Some boats even carried zoos and museums! Often, the show was held right on the boat. Other times, the showboat pulled a flat boat, called a barge, behind it. Then the theater was on the barge.

What was the first steamship to cross the Atlantic?

The paddle-wheel boat *Savannah* crossed the ocean in 1819. It left its home in Georgia and headed for Liverpool, England. Although many people believed that such a "steam coffin" would never make it all the way across the Atlantic Ocean, the *Savannah* made it to England—29 days later!

Twenty-nine days was not a record time for a ship to cross the Atlantic. Any packet ship of the day could have made the trip in that amount of time—or even less. Why wasn't the *Savannah's* trip faster? The reason is that the *Savannah* was built as a sailing ship. A steam engine and paddle wheels were added later. Most of the first Atlantic crossing was made using sail power. The *Savannah* had only enough fuel to run its engine for about 85 hours. The *Savannah's* trip was a first—but only a small beginning for steam.

When was the first all-steam ocean crossing?

The first all-steam crossing took place 19 years later, in 1838. The *Sirius* (SIR-ee-us) made the trip from Ireland to the east coast of the United States in 18½ days. By the 1840s, many steamships were making trips across the Atlantic Ocean.

Why don't we see paddle-wheel boats anymore?

The paddle wheel was replaced by the propeller. Starting in 1816, propellers were installed in some boats. Others still had paddle wheels. Great arguments took place as to which was better. In 1845, races were held between two nearly identical British ships, the *Rattler* and the *Alecto*. The *Rattler* had a propeller; the *Alecto* had a paddle wheel. The *Rattler* won every race! Soon after that, propellers replaced paddle wheels.

MODERN STEAMSHIPS

What do steamships look like today?

You have probably seen pictures of huge ocean liners such as the *Queen Elizabeth 2*. You may even have seen the actual liners. You can recognize them by their large smokestacks. Most ships with smokestacks are steamships, but some have diesel engines, and others use atomic energy.

Queen Elizabeth 2

How long does it take a steamship to cross the ocean today?

A fast steamship can cross the Atlantic Ocean between New York and Southampton, England, in 5½ days. It takes about 12 days for a steamship to cross the Pacific Ocean from Seattle, Washington, to Kobe, Japan.

What is it like to travel on a modern ocean liner?

A modern ocean liner is like a floating hotel. Once on board, it's easy to forget you're on a ship. The rooms are something like hotel rooms, and every modern convenience is right at your fingertips. There are restaurants, shops, game rooms, elevators, gymnasiums, swimming pools, and theaters.

NOW THIS IS THE LIFE!

CHAPTER 4

From motor boats to cargo ships to ferries, boats have many different uses. Do you hear the whistle blowing? Three toots means Snoopy and the *Peanuts* gang are ready to shove off for a tour of boats, large and small.

BOATS ON PARADE

THE BEAGLE

THE ALL-PURPOSE MOTORBOAT

What is a motorboat?

A motorboat is the type of boat you see most often on lakes and rivers and in marinas—basins of water in which boats are docked. A motorboat is used for fun, fishing, transportation, rescue operations, police patrols, and even water-skiing. Motorboats come in many different sizes, just like sailboats. Motorboats have either an outboard motor or an inboard engine to make them move. An outboard motor is one attached to the outside of a boat. An inboard engine is one built right into the boat. The sailor uses a steering wheel to make turns.

BOATS FOR FUN

PEDAL FASTER, SCHROEDER. WE HAVE TO CATCH THAT SPEED BOAT!

What is a pedal boat?

A pedal boat is a cross between a bicycle and a boat. Pedal boats have no motors or sails or paddles. They have two seats and foot pedals. Pedal boats don't move quickly. They are usually made of plastic and are used only for fun.

The sleek design of this racing boat allows it to cut through the water at high speeds.

What is a cigarette boat?

Originally, "Cigarette" was the brand name of one of the first superfast powerboats. Today, it has come to mean any thin, fast sportboat. These boats usually measure between 20 and 45 feet in length. Cigarette boats are made of lightweight fiberglass and may be powered by three engines. Their needle-nose design cuts down drag, allowing some cigarette boats to reach speeds of 100 miles per hour.

What are some features of cruising yachts?

Cruising yachts trade speed for comfort and seaworthiness. All the comforts of home—from sleeping bunks to a kitchen—can be found on most larger cruising yachts. Today's yachts also have the most modern sailing instruments such as radar and long-range radio communication (up to 400 miles) to help navigate, or steer, the boat.

CARGO SHIPS

STAND ASIDE, SWABBIE... A CAPTAIN HAS IMPORTANT DUTIES TO ATTEND!

What is a cargo ship?

A cargo ship carries goods for trading. The old clipper ships were cargo ships, carrying tea and spices from China to the United States. They needed to be fast so that the cargo would not spoil before it could be unloaded. Today, many cargo ships have refrigerators on them.

Modern cargo ships are divided into four categories according to the things they carry. General cargo ships carry things that are put in packages, such as food, machinery, and clothing. Tankers carry oil or other liquids. Dry bulk carriers carry un-packaged goods such as coal or grain. Multipurpose ships can carry several different kinds of cargo at once.

Large electric cranes lift boxes and barrels onto and off of cargo ships. Once the cargo is aboard, crew members store it.

What is a supertanker?

A supertanker is a very large oil-carrying tanker. Except for some ships in the military, supertankers are the biggest ships. They are often longer than three football fields in a row! Supertankers are slower than other types of large ships, but they provide the cheapest way to carry oil. The liquid cargo that tanker ships carry is pumped on and off the tanker through special hoses.

A supertanker can travel only through large, deep bodies of water.

BARGES, TUGBOATS, FIREBOATS, AND FERRIES

What is a barge?

A barge is a flat-bottomed boat used to carry heavy freight, such as coal or steel. It usually has square ends that make docking and unloading easy.

In the old days, barges had no motors. They were pulled by horses or oxen. The animals would walk on the land next to the river or canal, pulling ropes attached to the barge. Now this towing work is usually done by tugboats. Some modern barges have their own motors. These barges can carry up to 20 million pounds of freight.

These tugboats are hard at work pulling an oil rig setup out to sea.

What are tugboats?

Tugboats are small, powerful boats. They are used to tow and guide bigger boats and ships into or out of a harbor. Tugs are used to pull large ocean liners and cargo ships through shallow waters or narrow areas. Without the tugs, large ships have a hard time moving through such small places. Some tugboats tow damaged ships into harbors.

Modern tugboats get their power from diesel engines. In the 1800s, tugs were driven by steam-powered paddle wheels.

What is a fireboat?

A fireboat puts out fires on ships and piers. It is like a fire engine on the water. Most big ports have at least one fireboat. Fireboats are equipped with powerful water guns that shoot great streams of water at the fire. A nozzle at the top of a tall tower shoots water the farthest. It can aim water at the deck or the inside of a burning ship. When big passenger liners come into a harbor, fireboats sometimes greet them by spraying water high into the air.

What is a ferry?

A ferry is a boat that carries people across a small body of water, such as a lake or a river. Some ferries carry people over larger bodies of water. However, all ferries travel back and forth between two ports on a regular schedule. Some ferry rides take five minutes. Others take two days. The ferries that make long trips have dining rooms and sleeping compartments.

This ferry runs between the state of Washington and its neighboring islands, the San Juan Islands.

Often, people bring bicycles on ferries. Larger ferries allow people to bring their cars, and some ferries are even large enough to carry railroad trains. Those ferries have their own tracks. That way, a whole train can ride right onto a train ferry and then ride off again. Most ferries are run by diesel or steam engines. In some places, however, ferries are pushed along with poles, or pulled by people or animals on a nearby shore or riverbank.

MILITARY SHIPS

What are today's military ships like?

From submarines that run silently deep under the water to ships that glide above it, today's military ships come in all shapes and sizes. The U.S. Navy's fleet includes 669 ships of war and 640 submarines. There are cruisers that launch guided missiles, aircraft carriers that can carry as many as 80 planes, and battleships that can use their guns to hit targets hundreds of miles away.

These warships use modern technology such as computers and advanced radar systems to spot their enemies. Many of them also use nuclear power, which allows them to go hundreds of thousands of miles without refueling.

42

What is "Old Ironsides"?

"Old Ironsides" is the nickname for a battleship called the *Constitution*. It had 44 guns and was one of the first warships of the United States. The *Constitution* won more battles than any other ship. It fought most of its famous battles during the War of 1812. Throughout all its fights, the hull was never damaged. That is why the ship was called "Old Ironsides."

Women were not allowed to work on the *Constitution* when it was a battle-ship. A woman named Lucy Brewer didn't like that. She dressed up in men's clothing and fooled the Marines!

When did a plane first take off from a ship?

In 1910, an American pilot named Eugene Ely launched a plane from a boat. Using a ramp built on the navy cruiser U.S.S. *Birmingham*, Ely flew his plane two and a half miles from the ship to a soft ground landing.

From above, this aircraft carrier looks like a floating airport!

What is an aircraft carrier?

An aircraft carrier is a huge military ship that carries aircraft. Planes can take off from and land on its deck. This floating airport helps navies use planes to find and attack enemy ships. A carrier has a runway on top and a flight deck below for storing and repairing planes.

WE LUCYS HAVE ALWAYS BEEN ABLE TO GET OUR WAY!

BOATS FROM FARAWAY PLACES

What are gondolas?

Gondolas are long, thin rowboats often used as water taxis. They are popular in Venice, Italy. Instead of roads, most of Venice has canals—narrow inland waterways. People there use boats instead of cars.

At the back of a gondola stands the gondolier—the person who runs the boat. The gondolier uses a long pole to push the gondola.

A junk sits in the waters off Hong Kong.

What is a junk?

A junk is a kind of wooden sailboat. It was first used by the Chinese a few hundred years ago. If you go to the Orient today, you will still see many junks. They are usually painted in bright colors. White circles on the front stand for eyes. People who sail junks believe that these eyes are the boats' guiding spirits that watch for danger.

Junks have flat bottoms and high sterns. The stern is the back of a boat. Junks have two or more four-cornered sails. Compared to modern boats, junks are slow, so some people put motors on their junks.

Hong Kong is famous for its crowded sampan city.

What is a sampan?

A sampan is a small, fast-moving boat found chiefly in China, Japan, and other countries in the Orient. They are also used in India and on many islands in the Pacific Ocean.

A sampan is usually flat-bottomed. Often this type of boat is used as a house for a family. Some sampans are also used for carrying freight or products to be sold at market. Not all sampans look alike, but most have an arched or boxed cabin covered with straw mats. A cabin is the place on the boat where people live.

Most sampans are equipped with both oars and sails. If there's no wind for sailing, the owners can always row the boat.

Where is there a floating sampan "city"?

In Hong Kong, a city on the south coast of China, groups of people live and work on sampans docked right next to each other. Some sampans are homes. Others are food stores and restaurants. Many of the sampans are very old. Their cabin covers are full of patches.

45

Some boats don't exactly float. They skim over the water or glide on ice or travel beneath the sea. Let's hop on board with the *Peanuts* gang for some oceangoing fun!

IS THAT REALLY A BOAT?

BOATS ABOVE THE WATER

What is a hydrofoil?

A hydrofoil is a boat that skims very quickly over the water. Its hull stays just above the surface. Only the hydrofoil's "sea wings" stay in the water. These work very much like airplane wings. When a plane picks up speed, the wings lift it into the air. In the same way, when the hydrofoil picks up speed, its sea wings lift it out of the water. There is less drag from the water, so the hydrofoil can travel much faster than other kinds of boats. Hydrofoils are used for passenger travel and by the military.

This hydrofoil can move faster because of the red "sea wings" beneath its hull.

A hovercraft whizzes over the surface of the water!

What is a hovercraft?

A hovercraft is also called an air-cushioned vehicle (ACV). It can be driven on water or land. It has fans or propellers that take in air at the top and blow it out the bottom. A hovercraft is lifted above the surface of the water by the air that comes out under it. These amazing vehicles shouldn't really be called boats, since they travel above the surface of the water, not in it. A hovercraft can go almost anywhere—swamps, mud, river rapids, even over ice.

A sailor keeps his iceboat balanced as it speeds across the ice.

What is an iceboat?

An iceboat is a narrow, pointed sailboat that travels on ice instead of on water. It can do this because it rests on runners—usually three. They look something like short skis. An iceboat's sails are usually very large. They catch the wind and make the iceboat move, just as they would any sailboat.

Iceboating (also called ice yachting) has long been a favorite pastime in Norway, Sweden, Denmark, and Finland. There, the water is frozen much of the year. Today, iceboating is a popular winter sport in many other countries, as well.

What is an icebreaker?

An icebreaker is a special kind of ship designed to break through ice. Its bow is covered with strong metal that acts as armor. An icebreaker has propellers both in back and in front. This makes the ship easier to handle. To break the ice, the ship's bow climbs partly up onto the ice. The weight of the ship causes the ice to break. In order to push the heavy ship onto the ice, the icebreaker's engines must be very powerful.

SUBMARINES

Are any other boats good for traveling in icy places?

Yes. Submarines—called subs for short—can travel where ice usually stops most ships. Submarines go underneath the ice. By traveling under it, a nuclear submarine named the *Nautilus* reached the North Pole in 1958. The next year, a nuclear sub named the *Skate* broke through the North Pole ice.

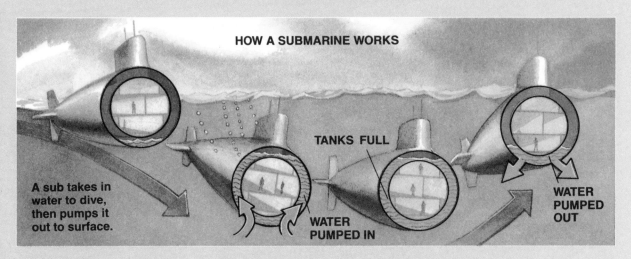

HOW A SUBMARINE WORKS

TANKS FULL

A sub takes in water to dive, then pumps it out to surface.

WATER PUMPED IN

WATER PUMPED OUT

How else are submarines used?

Oceanographers (o-shun-OG-ruh-furz) are scientists who study ocean life. They use submarines to explore the bottom of the sea, and to help them get valuable minerals from the ocean floor. Small submarines, called submersibles, are used to explore sunken ships.

How does a submarine go up and down?

In order to dive, or go down, a submarine takes water into special storage tanks. The water adds weight to a submarine. When the sub gets heavy enough, it sinks. To surface, or go up, air is forced into the tanks, and the water is blown out. The submarine now rises to the surface of the sea. It will stay on the surface until the tanks are filled with water again.

Once underwater, a sub can move up or down by using steel fins at the rear of the ship. These are called diving planes. When the fins are tilted down, the submarine will dive. When they are tilted up, the sub will rise.

What were the first subs like?

Early submarine experiments date back hundreds of years. In the 1620s, a Dutch engineer named Cornelius Drebbel built the first submarine. It was a leather-covered rowing boat that could travel underwater. Twelve men with oars sat inside and rowed. The inventor used a chemical to keep the air breathable, but he kept the formula a secret, so no one knows what the chemical was.

The first sub ever used in a war was called the *Turtle*. It was used in 1776 during the American Revolution. It attacked a British warship, but the attack was not successful. The British ship did not sink. The *Turtle* was shaped something like a turtle's shell. A man sat inside and turned a pole called a crankshaft. The crankshaft was attached to propellers. When the crankshaft moved, the propellers moved. Then the sub moved.

Where did breathable air come from in later submarines?

In the early 1900s, submarines could stay underwater only for short periods of time. The subs did not have any way to replace air. The problem was solved with a snorkel. This was a tube that came out of the top of the sub. It allowed fresh air to come into the cabin. With snorkels, subs could travel for long periods just below the surface of the water. They could not stay in deep water, however, for more than a few hours at a time.

Today, subs make their own oxygen from seawater, so they can stay underwater for a long time.

What kind of power do submarines use today?

Modern submarines use nuclear energy. It is the most powerful force known. Uranium (you-RAY-nee-um) is the fuel used for nuclear energy. One ounce of it gives out as much energy as is created by burning 100 tons of coal, so nuclear-powered subs can travel long distances without refueling.

I HATE IT WHEN WOODSTOCK PLAYS SUBMARINE IN MY WATER DISH!

Are any ships besides submarines powered by nuclear energy?

As we learned, nuclear energy has been used in a few, mostly military, U.S. and Soviet ships. Nuclear power for civilian ships is still in the experimental stage. The equipment needed is very bulky, and it's also very expensive. That's why most ships today are powered by diesel or steam engines.

A submarine moves slowly through ocean waters.

THE DIVING BELL

What's the deepest anyone has ever gone in the ocean?

Nearly 36,000 feet is the deepest. Since the sixteenth century, scientists have used diving bells—round, airtight containers—to go underwater. In 1960, two men went down 35,817 feet into the Pacific Ocean. They reached the deepest known part of the ocean. The long trip down took more than five hours and was made in a diving bell called a bathyscaphe (BATH-ih-skaff). A bathyscaphe carries heavy steel to make it sink. When the steel is dropped, the bathyscaphe gets lighter and comes up. Early diving bells were lowered into the water on heavy ropes or steel cables. Bathyscaphes carry oxygen in bottles, and chemicals for cleaning used air.

CHAPTER 6

ANCHORS AWEIGH!

An ocean is a very big place indeed. It stretches as far as the eye can see and seems like an easy place in which to get lost. Well, let's join Captain Charlie Brown and his mates to see how ships set sail and come back again, safe and sound, and without getting lost.

THE CAPTAIN'S LOG

Why does a ship's captain keep a log book?

A ship's log is the daily record of a trip. The ship's captain is usually the one who keeps the log. The captain writes down all the important details of the trip. These include the exact route, events that happen on board, and radio messages. Over the years, ships' log books have been a great help in piecing together facts about the history of sea travel. A log is also important if a ship has an accident. It helps uncover the reason for the mishap.

MAPS, COMPASSES, RADAR, AND SOUND WAVES

Does a ship's captain have a road map to follow?

Yes, in a way. A ship's captain has the help of one or more specially trained people called navigators. Before beginning a voyage, the navigators mark the ship's route on a special sea map, called a chart. During the trip, they keep track of the ship's position by using radar and other electronic equipment. The captain uses this information to stay on the course marked on the chart.

In ancient times, sailors figured out their direction by looking at the stars. By the 1100s, sailors were using compasses to tell direction.

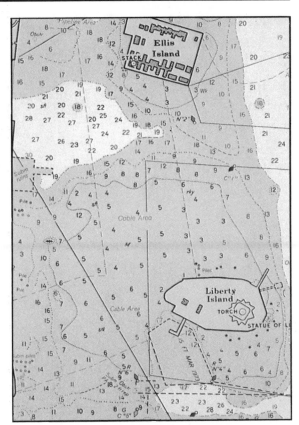

Charts such as this one help navigators mark a ship's route.

How does a compass work?

A compass needle is a magnet. The Earth's North and South poles also are magnets. If a compass needle is free to turn, it lines itself up with the Earth's magnetic poles. One end points toward the north. The other end points toward the south.

Letters painted on a dial under the needle show all the directions. A sailor just has to look at the compass to see which way the ship is going. For example, if the north end of the compass needle points toward the back of the ship, that means north is behind it. The ship is traveling south.

How does radar help ships?

The word *radar* stands for **ra**dio **d**etecting **an**d **r**anging. It is a way of telling direction and distance by using radio waves. A radar antenna sends out special signals called radio waves. When these waves bump into a solid object, they bounce back to the antenna. The radar device measures the time it takes for the waves to travel back and forth. Then it figures out where the object is.

Radar will warn a ship's captain—even in fog—of something in the way of the ship.

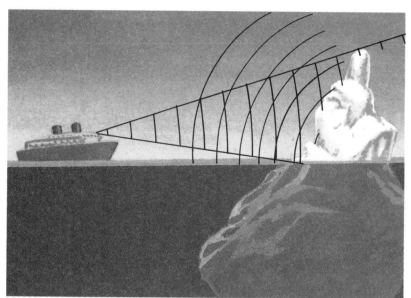

Radio waves sent by a ship's radar bump into an iceberg and bounce back to the ship's antenna. Now the ship won't run into the iceberg!

How do sound waves help ships?

Sailors can't see the floor of the ocean, so they use sound to help them get a picture of it. An instrument called a depth sounder sends a high-pitched sound that travels to the ocean bottom. From there, its echo bounces back to the surface. The depth sounder measures how long it takes for the echo to bounce back. If it takes a long time, it means that the echo had to bounce back a long distance and that the water is deep. This process is called *sonar*, which stands for **so**und **na**vigation **r**anging. Some depth sounders not only tell the depth of the water, they also use echoes to detect fish!

DOCKING THE BOAT

What is an anchor?

An anchor is a heavy metal object attached to the boat by a long rope or chain. When the anchor is thrown overboard, its pointed hook digs into the bottom of the ocean, river, or lake. It keeps the boat from drifting away. Before leaving a boat, a good sailor pulls on the anchor to make sure it has a firm hold in the ground. Boats need anchors unless they are tied to a dock.

The famous oceanographer Jacques Cousteau (ZHOCK koo-STOE) dropped an anchor 24,600 feet into the Atlantic Ocean!

How are boats docked?

A small boat is easy to dock. The skipper, or captain, just slows the boat down and heads for the dock at an angle. Because the boat is moving so slowly, it rubs up next to the dock very gently. Sometimes bumpers on the dock or boat give extra protection. Once the boat is docked, the skipper jumps off and ties it up.

A big ship is harder to dock. While a harbor pilot steers the ship, a tugboat pushes it into place. Many people are needed to help tie up the ship.

What is a harbor pilot?

When a ship comes into or leaves a harbor, a harbor pilot must be on board. His job is to guide the ship through the harbor. The pilot is familiar with the tides, the winds, and all the specially shaped or marked floats in the water. Such floating markers are called buoys (BOO-ees).

What is the difference between a port and a harbor?

Sometimes people use the words *port* and *harbor* to mean the same thing, but there is a difference. All ports are harbors, but not all harbors are ports.

A harbor is a part of the body of water that is deep enough for anchoring boats or ships. A harbor is partly surrounded by land, or else it has piers that extend into the water. The land or the piers protect boats from strong winds and currents and rough water. A port is a special kind of harbor. Passengers and freight can be loaded or unloaded there. A large, busy port usually has cranes for handling heavy freight, warehouses for storing things, radio equipment, repair services, fueling stations, and even restaurants.

What are buoys used for?

Buoys help sailors find their way in strange waters. Most buoys are used as channel markers. A channel is the bottom of a body of water. Channel markers warn sailors of shallow or rocky areas in the water or give other important information. Some buoys are used to anchor boats.

AHOY!

DRY DOCK

This large ship is in dry dock to be repaired.

What are dry docks?

In order for a ship to be repaired and painted, it must be taken out of the water. Since large ships are heavy, special docks called dry docks were invented. There are two main kinds, the floating dock and the graving dock.

What is a floating dock?

A floating dry dock is a floating platform with walls on two sides. Water is pumped into it. The dock sinks, and the ship moves onto it. When the water is pumped out again, the dock rises once more to the surface. Now the ship is in dry dock and ready for repair.

What is a graving dock?

A graving dry dock is a deep concrete tub sunk into the ground. One end of it opens into the harbor. When the ship enters, a gate closes the tub off from the harbor. Then, as the water is pumped out, the ship sinks to the bottom of the tub. When all the water is out, the ship is in dry dock.

The Unsinkable *Titanic*

The *Titanic* was the largest ocean liner in the world when it was built. Experts said that the ship would never sink, but on its very first trip, the *Titanic* hit an iceberg and sank. The lifeboats could hold only half of the people on the ship, so many people drowned. The wreck is still at the bottom of the ocean.

Using a submersible—an underwater vehicle— called *Alvin*, scientists recently discovered the wreck. *Alvin* was able to dive 13,000 feet, much deeper than other submersibles had gone. With the help of a camera, the rest of the world was able to see photographs of the *Titanic's* ballroom, complete with chandelier, railing, and a bottle of champagne!

ALVIN, COME BACK!

Jet Set

It's a scooter! It's a water jet! No, it's just a super jet ski, a cross between a motorcycle and water skis. An engine draws water in from under the jet ski, then blows it out the back. This stream pushes the jet ski through the water very quickly. The jet ski has a platform on the back where the rider can lie down, kneel, or stand.

This is one vehicle you'll never lose. If you fall off, the jet ski turns slowly in a circle, giving you a chance to catch your breath and swim back to it.

A jet skier guides her jet ski into a turn.

IF YOU'RE HUNGRY AND YOU REALLY WANT YOUR SUPPER, YOU HAVE TO KNOW HOW TO STARE AT THE BACK DOOR...

YOUR EYES HAVE TO FLASH LIKE THE BEACON FROM A LIGHTHOUSE!

A GOOD STARE CAN PEEL THE PAINT RIGHT OFF THE DOOR!

5-10

© 1989 United Feature Syndicate, Inc

Night Lights

The lights and signals from lighthouses help sailors steer their ships in the right direction. Lightships are floating lighthouses that are permanently anchored near the shore. Their powerful lights and foghorns warn sailors of nearby hazards such as rocks or shallow water.

Computer Sailing

A French sailing ship called the *Wind Song* uses a computer to control its sails. There are four masts on this large sailboat. At 440 feet long, it is the longest sailboat used today.

Getting to the Bottom

Ships called dredges have special digging tools. They bring up mud and gravel from the bottom of oceans, rivers, or lakes. Dredges are used to make shipping channels deeper and wider so large vessels can get through. They are also used to dig for valuable minerals or to build up land along the shore.

Tied in Knots?

Instead of giving speed in "miles per hour," sailors refer to "knots." A knot equals 1.15 miles per hour. To change from miles per hour to knots, divide by 1.15. For example, 38 miles per hour is the same speed as 33 knots.

MY BRAIN GETS TIED IN KNOTS JUST TRYING TO UNDERSTAND THAT!

IN THE
NEXT VOLUME

Have you ever wondered how trick-or-treating got started, or why we eat turkey on Thanksgiving, or who decorated the first Christmas tree? You can find answers to these questions and lots more in volume 11, *Holidays Around the World—Let's Celebrate!*